Flood!

The Brentford Flood of 1841

Valerie Bott

Brentford & Chiswick
Local History Society

This first edition published by
Brentford & Chiswick Local History Society 2002
3 Campden Terrace, Linden Gardens, London W4 2EP

Set in Gill Sans
Designed by Toni Marshall
Printed by West 4 Printers Ltd

ISBN 0-9508025-0-6

Introduction & Acknowledgments

It is now some years since Mary Prior, author of *Fisher Row – Fishermen, Bargemen & Canal Boatmen in Oxford 1500-1900* (OUP 1982), gave me her notes of a report from Jackson's Oxford Journal describing the Brentford Flood in January 1841. This set me investigating a poignant story of a community coping with loss and severe damage, finding resources to support each other, to help the most needy – including the outsiders stranded in their midst – and to get back in business. In unravelling it I have learnt a great deal about the town of Brentford at the beginning of Victoria's reign and found parallels with some more recent disasters.

The original material directly relating to the Flood is limited and as a result I have had to rely upon contemporary newspaper reports, particularly those in The Times newspaper. I have read and re-read these, asking questions about what they said – and sometimes about what they did not say. It has taken some time to answer enough of these questions to make it possible to produce more than just a modern version of the story written by Victorian journalists. Moreover, the enthusiasm of local audiences when they have heard me talk about the Brentford Flood has encouraged me to write this account.

I am grateful to a number of people and organisations who helped me a great deal. Andrea Cameron and Carolyn Hammond, local studies librarians with the London Borough of Hounslow, found contemporary newscuttings, census material, maps and illustrations from the local collection. The Hounslow Library Network has generously given me permission for the use of illustrations and the documents about the disaster fund. Elizabeth Wood of the Society for Sailing Barge Research assisted enormously by investigating the details of barge owners from her own research notes and from the manuscript lists of the Watermen's Company in the Guildhall Library.

Material about the Welsh Harp reservoir came from the Grange Museum (L B Brent), of which I was Keeper when I began to research the flood in the early 1980s; thanks go to the Brent Archive for permission to reproduce the photograph of the reservoir dam. The Waterways Museum in Stoke Bruerne found me the print of the wrecks issued by E Wildman immediately after the flood and gave permission for its reproduction here. Subsequently I discovered that Hounslow also has copies of this print, as well as two watercolours (one wrongly annotated 1840) based upon it, and a very melodramatic illustration of the "Awful Inundation at Brentford" published in February 1841.

Information about the weather in the winter of 1840/41 including details of records kept by the Royal Horticultural Society, was provided by the Meteorological Office at Bracknell in Berkshire and details of the tides on the night of the flood came from the Hydrographic Office of the Ministry of Defence at Taunton. The records of the Grand Junction Canal Company in the Public Record Office provided details of the company's actions and decisions in the months after the flood.

Thanks go to Gill Clegg and Janet McNamara for advice, information and ideas, to James Wisdom for his encouragement and to the Brentford & Chiswick Local History Society for publishing this book.

Valerie Bott
May 2002

The Brentford Flood – January 1841

On the night of 16/17 January 1841, a major disaster hit the market town of Brentford in Middlesex. After some weeks of freezing weather there had been a sudden thaw resulting in very serious flooding and considerable damage. Several people lost their lives and many became homeless. This is an account of what appears to have happened on that night and the ways in which people coped. Much of the story is told in the words of contemporary newspaper reports but other sources have been used where they make it possible to verify or to expand the information these provide.

The second half of the 20th century saw a number of disasters around the world, some natural, such as earthquakes, floods and avalanches, and some where human error or technical failure have contributed to the sinking of passenger vessels and to rail and aeroplane crashes. The winters of 2000/1 and 2001/2 saw very heavy rainfall and flooding in many English towns. All of this has been photographed, filmed and videoed, reported in the next day's newspapers and broadcast almost instantly into our homes, even if the events took place on the other side of the world. We know what such disasters look like and that speedy assistance, both practical and financial, is needed.

The people of Brentford did not have such wide knowledge or experience to draw upon, though the news of their plight travelled quickly, with press stories appearing within 36 hours of the disaster. The best reports appear in *The Times*. No other incident of comparable significance relating to the locality was reported in this major newspaper between 1800 and 1851. The reports are formal rather than sensational, with a wealth of detail as to how resources were found quickly to support those who were suffering, as local grandees rallied round, shelter was provided and fund-raising began. Human nature being much the same in 1841 as it is today, sightseers appeared in large numbers almost immediately and squabbles arose about the priorities for action.

Like all newspaper reports, these may have their inaccuracies, but they do have an immediacy which arises from both the reporter's close observation and from the sense of direct involvement in the accounts of those who witnessed or suffered from the Flood. The reports have been written by the journalist, so they may not use exactly the words of those who were there. For example, while the policemen may have been accustomed to giving formal reports of incidents for a trial or an inquest, the others certainly would not. So a young man recently escaped from the terror of that night was unlikely to refer to his colleague from another boat as "the deceased" unless he was caught up in the formality of the language of the coroner. However, some of the reports have a strong sense of being direct testimony from those who were there.

Brentford in 1841

Brentford grew up close to the point where the Brent flows into the Thames and where first a ford and later a bridge carried the main (Roman) road west out of London over the Brent. By the time of the Flood the built-up High Street extended from Kew Bridge into Isleworth, with a little community just west of Brentford Bridge known as Brentford End. Across the Thames lay the royal estate we know as Kew Gardens and, to the west, across the Brent, the Duke of Northumberland's Syon House estate in Isleworth Parish.

The Half Acre and Boston Lane mark the boundary between two elements of the town. Old Brentford, to the east, was originally part of the parish of Ealing, and New Brentford, originally part of Hanwell Parish, lay between these roads and the Brent. The town had prospered for centuries, and "New" Brentford had acquired its name in the middle ages. This was a market town with its own fairs and excellent shops. It also provided for travellers passing through by road or water. Like today's motorway service stations, it offered food, drink, accommodation in numerous inns, and stabling and farriers for the horses. The railway did not reach Brentford until the end of the 1840s and Brentford Dock, straddling the boundary between New Brentford and Isleworth Parishes, was not opened by the Great Western Railway until 1859.

By the time of the flood Brentford's population was around 10,000[1] and growing rapidly. Around the town, particularly to the north and west, were significant market gardens, nurseries and orchards serving the London market. The 1801 census recorded 272 houses in New Brentford alone; by

---

[1] Pigot & Co's 1839 Directory of Middlesex refers to the 1831 census as recording 2,085 inhabitants in New Brentford and 7,783 in Old Brentford, totalling 9,868.

1851 there were 389 in New Brentford and a further 1,750 in what was now referred to as "Brentford Town" in Old Brentford. Though there were some substantial houses, especially around the Butts, most inhabitants occupied tiny cottages crammed together in narrow yards and alleys, a number of which ran south of the High Street towards the riverside. There was extreme poverty and considerable wealth side by side.

By 1841 Brentford could boast a range of industries, with a gas works, a substantial soap factory, malt-houses and breweries, mills, a turpentine works, a tannery and a distillery. Along the banks of river and canal, boat-builders and barge owners were to be found, and wharves and substantial warehousing for grain, coal and timber. One of the oldest-established mills was on the River Brent on the west side of The Butts. Though it was not demolished until the early 1900s, it does not figure in the description of the disaster, the lists of properties damaged or owners compensated. It seems likely that by this time it was semi-derelict, having been cut off by the creation of the canal.

"It is here that the Grand Junction Canal enters the Thames", said Pigot & Co's 1839 Directory of Middlesex, "from which circumstance, in addition to the great thoroughfare of the place, arises its present prosperity". Linking Braunston, in the Midlands, with London via the Thames at Brentford, the canal was built between 1794 and 1805. The Paddington Branch was added in 1801 and this in turn was later linked by means of the Regent's Canal to the Thames at Limehouse. It soon became clear that a reliable water supply was essential to maintain water levels in this busy canal system, so in the mid-1830s the river Brent was dammed at Kingsbury to create a reservoir which could store this water. Later known as the Welsh Harp, after a nearby pub, this attractive stretch of water can still be seen from the North Circular Road at Neasden.

Most of the damage caused by the Flood affected the homes and businesses lying closest to the waterways. For centuries the Brent entered the Thames across a delta, the main channel of which was improved to become the canal, with a lock close to the confluence of the two rivers. When the Flood occurred this flat land was overwhelmed by the huge flow of water which sought the most natural route towards the Thames.

The winter of 1840 to 1841

This appears to have been an exceptionally harsh winter. The Royal Horticultural Society, then established with gardens in the neighbouring parish of Chiswick, kept detailed weather records which confirm its severity. Their published tables include the following summary: "This month has proved colder than any December experienced in the present century, the mean temperature exactly corresponding with the freezing point. North-east winds were prevalent and the deposition from rain and melted snow was very little. Thick hoar frosts and fog were general in the last week. On the 25th in particular the fog was very dense all day, and the frost at night severe. By the end of the month, the frost had penetrated to the depth of 8 inches in kitchen garden soil and in turf about 4 inches."

So the freezing weather, the days of heavy rain and the sudden thaw combined to create the circumstances of the disastrous flood at Brentford

In January they recorded that "the mean temperature was about 2° below the average for this month. On the nights of the 7th and 8th the frost was intense, the thermometer falling to within 6° of zero. The barometer was considerably below the average and the depth of rain was more than an inch above the usual quantity. A tremendous thunderstorm occurred on the 3rd, about 7am, accompanied at first with high wind and then hail and sleet, the flashes of lightning being unusually large and vivid. Much rain and snow fell between the 10th and the 15th; a rapid thaw took place on the 16th, the water at the same time being prevented from sinking into the earth by the frozen crust, which was from 8 to 12 inches in depth where the ground was bare; the consequences were great inundations throughout the country with loss of life and property."

Newspaper reports in the third week of January mentioned flooding in Windsor (the playing fields of Eton College were under 3 or 4 feet of water) and Cambridge, as well as a number of incidents of flood damage in Middlesex. These included the palings around the grounds of the County Lunatic Asylum at Hanwell being thrown down by the water and thirty-two sheep being washed away from Twyford Abbey, of which two had been found drowned. At Hayes and at Uxbridge the high road was under water for some days and Mr Stevens' mill and residence at Uxbridge were under water. The sudden thaw meant the surface ice and snow began to melt, but the frozen ground would have taken longer to warm up and could not absorb the water.

One factor which fortunately did not make matters worse in January 1841 was the state of the tide on the Thames. The Admiralty Tide Tables for January 1841 give predictions of the state of the tide from which we can calculate that at the worst stages of the disaster, between 3 and 5 am, the tide would have been at low water. The heavy rain of the previous few days and the rapid thaw immediately before the flood, could well have meant that the Thames was very full, carrying water down from its upper reaches as well as from the immediate locality, but the level and flow of the Thames do not appear to have been a significant factor and are not mentioned in the reports of inquests.

The events of the night of 16/17 January 1841

So the freezing weather, the days of heavy rain and the sudden thaw combined to create the circumstances of the disastrous flood at Brentford. And the presence of the waterways so close to the heart of the town not only made the impact of the flood severe but also made the people who depended upon the waterways for their livelihood the main victims. Newspaper reports provide very detailed accounts of the event from 18 January onwards, at first daily and then at longer intervals into February, as relief was provided and inquests held.

The best description by far is that which appeared in *The Times* on 18 January 1841; other newspapers, such as *Jackson's Oxford Journal* and the *Gardeners' Chronicle*, used large extracts of this text as their own in the following days. Writing in rather formal English, the reporter's long sentences convey something of his breathlessness as he described an astonishing scene. He had

"...immediately hastened to the scene of the devastation, which he reached between 11 and 12 o'clock of the forenoon. On entering New Brentford he found the town crowded by persons from all the neighbouring parts. The waters had by that time materially subsided, yet the high-road was for some distance covered by large blocks of ice, some nearly a foot in thickness, which had been left behind by the receding waters, whilst the inhabitants of the houses on both sides of the road were busily employed with the town fire engine and portable pumps of every description, endeavouring to draw water from their houses."

He found at that time that things were so confused and people so excitable that it was hard to get accurate details of the true extent of the damage to property and people, and the loss of life. However, he did manage to talk to some people who had actually witnessed the events of the previous night and wrote the following account. (In this description, the "barges" are the sailing vessels carrying goods on the Thames while the "monkey boats" are the narrow boats, the familiar trading vessels of the canal.)

"The water, it appears, was first observed to be slowly rising about half past 12 o'clock on Saturday night, but no fears of an inundation being entertained by the persons residing near, they retired to rest, little dreaming that they would be so soon aroused from their slumbers. Towards 2 o'clock, however, Police-constable Smith T60, who was on duty near the bridge, observing the water still increasing and rushing with great force to the Thames, awakened some of the boatmen belonging to what are called monkey boats, large numbers of which were moored off the different wharves abutting on the canal, and cautioned them to be on the alert for their own security.

At that time, and even up to half past 3 o'clock yesterday morning, immediate danger was not apprehended, but a few minutes before 4 o'clock a loud noise was heard to the north of the town which momentarily approached nearer and nearer, and it was soon ascertained that the narrow stream of the Brent had swelled into a mighty river, and overflowing its banks, was pouring itself into the already increased waters of the canal. Numbers of boats, barges and lighters were instantly torn from their moorings, and driven with great force through the bridge towards the Thames. At the same instant, also, the accumulated waters having overflowed all the premises north of the high-road burst with frightful force through two avenues by the houses of Mr Brasher, near the bridge, and Mr Farrell, directly opposite the church, filling the lower rooms of the houses.

The police immediately sprang

Men, women and children, many of them in their night clothes, were running in all directions for places of shelter, while the screams of the inhabitants were most appalling

their rattles, and lost no time in awakening the inhabitants to a sense of their danger, and where some were too deeply buried in sleep to be aroused by the knocking, they forced the doors open. The scene at that moment it is impossible to describe. Men, women and children, many of them in their night clothes, were running in all directions for places of shelter, while the roaring of the water, added to the screams of the wretched inhabitants of the boats, and of the individuals inhabiting the numerous cottages running south of the town down to the waterside, were most appalling.

In a very short time, all the occupiers of the houses near the market-place commenced damming up their doors, and there is no doubt that the whole not only of New Brentford, but also of Old Brentford, would shortly have become under water, had the stream not found itself an outlet at the bottom of Church Alley, by razing the wall of the extensive nursery grounds of Messrs Ronalds[2], and another wall at the southern extremity of the grounds, by which it joined the canal near its outlet to the Thames.

Every possible assistance was immediately rendered by those of the inhabitants who had not been reached by the inundation. At about 5 o'clock the water was at the highest, and the only means of communication between the houses near the bridge was by a boat. Towards 6 o'clock it was ascertained that the water was gradually decreasing, and daylight was anxiously looked for, that the extent of the effects of the inundation might be ascertained.

Above the bridge, as far as has been ascertained, the damage has not been so extensive as below it. Below the bridge, a short distance to the right, were found five large barges driven by the force of the water against the wharf of Mr Fowler, an extensive wharfinger at Brentford-end, and swamped, some lying over others. They belonged to Mr Charles Saunders, lighterman, and were laden with 1,300 quarters of corn and 350 quarters of linseed; but it was nearer to the mouth of the outlet of the Thames where

---

2 The Ronalds family, nurserymen and seedsmen, had been established in New Brentford from the middle of the 18th century. They operated nursery grounds behind Noy's House, between St Lawrence's Church and the Ham, and also between the Butts and Boston Manor Road, and they ran the Isleworth Nursery. Hugh Ronalds the younger specialised in fruit trees, growing 300 varieties of apple by 1829 and publishing *Pyrus Malus Brentfordiensis* in 1831. The plants may have survived the flooding, despite the demolition of the garden walls, as the Ronalds do not appear in the lists of those compensated.

the greatest damage has been done, and where a scene of ship-wreck unparalleled so far inland is still to be seen.

The spot in question is at the bottom of Boar's Head Yard, a turning leading from the high-road nearly opposite the market place, down to the canal. Off this spot the canal passes through some meadows, and there is a foot-bridge across it, and near that bridge are piled up craft of various descriptions to the number it is said of fifteen. There would no doubt have been more had not the pressure of the water forced down a large portion of the wall of the grounds of his Grace the Duke of Northumberland, by which the pent-up water obtained an outlet, carrying with it four or five barges, where they still remain. Some of these vessels are topsy-turvy, others are on their sides and portions of five can be distinctly seen above the water, piled on top of each other. It was impossible from the still great swell of the water yesterday, to ascertain to whom they belonged, the nature of their freight, or what had become of their crews; and it is feared that it will be ultimately found that several lives have been sacrificed."

Rescue bids & miraculous escapes

Few individuals are named in this first report of the flood apart from Police Constable Smith. He was clearly a very important figure that night, raising the alarm, awakening residents of houses and boats and, by acting promptly, saving lives. The 1841 Census records him living in Running Horse Yard in Brentford, aged 25, with his wife Emma who was 30. An anonymous newspaper cutting comments specifically upon the work of the local police, "The exertions of Inspector Marquand and the police of T division will not be soon effaced from the memory of the inhabitants". Smith's own account of the events appeared in *The Times* the following day:

"Our reporter has obtained from Police-constable Smith T60, who was on duty at the time at the side of the canal, the following statement of the occurrence:- It was about 20 minutes past 12 o'clock on Saturday, that he first noticed the boatmen whose boats were moored on the side of the canal preparatory to their departure, making remarks about the rising of the water, when he rendered them assistance in more securely fastening their craft. Before 1 o'clock, however, the ice broke up with a loud noise, when the boatmen became more alarmed, and some of them got out on the towing path, where they were immediately knee-deep in water, and one woman, about 2 o'clock, being knocked by a block of ice into the canal, he (Smith) jumped in and got her out

one woman, about 2 o'clock, being knocked by a block of ice into the canal, he jumped in and got her out.

About 2 o'clock a number of floats[3] belonging to Messrs Dowson & Co, which were moored at the entrance of the River Brent, got loose and he got into Messrs Dowson's yard and acquainted Mr Pepper, the manager, with the circumstances, who told him to tell the waterman of it, which, not being able to leave his boat he was unable to do.

He then went on to the bridge in the high road and watched the water, which kept gradually getting higher, until a few minutes before 4 o'clock, when the great body of water which hurried down the Brent forced into the canal, pouring over the locks without forcing them. They were instantly forced onward to the bridge where the first that sank was a coal barge. The next was one belonging to Mr Saunders, freighted with corn; then a coal barge belonging to Mr Eaton, and next one of Bessell's passage boats freighted with hoop iron, from which as it was sculling, he pulled up to the top of the bridge a child by means of his strap and also a woman, but before her husband could be got at the boat sank, and he swam on shore with great difficulty, and nearly lifeless.

Immediately afterwards another of Bessell's boats ran against the corner of Mr Whitehorn's house, and carried it away. As the boat passed under the bridge, Mr Plim, a butcher, threw a bullock rope to a woman who was on top of the cabin, who instantly seized hold of it and was partially drawn up, when, seeing her husband passing under the bridge without being rescued, she let go of it with one hand, but fortunately he (Smith) being at that moment sitting astride the parapet of the bridge, seized hold of her arm and she was saved. At that time, observing 14 or 15 women and children on the lock-bridge, he went and accompanied them to the lock-house, but admittance was refused[4] them; on which he got them onto

---

3 It is not clear exactly what these "floats" were. Joseph Dowson & Co were timber merchants with premises between the Brent and the High Street near the Tannery. The floats may have been substantial balks of timber stored in water of the old river Brent to aid the seasoning process. Alternatively they may have been small rafts or pontoons used in the firm's work. In both cases, the fact that they got loose helped to block the arch of the bridge.

4 A letter from W W Devereux, Toll Collector at the Canal Office, Brentford, appeared in *The Times* on 22 January. He disputed the report that admittance was refused: "Upon inquiry I cannot learn that any police constable even appeared at the lock-bridge as stated in your newspaper and am quite certain that neither a police constable nor any other person or persons, if they knocked, or called for, were not heard or refused admittance. [Neither] I myself, nor any of the inmates, was aware of the great danger in which we were placed until 4 o'clock, at which time it was impossible, from the strength of the current, for any person to approach us".

Brentford-bridge, here he knocked up the landlord of the Six Bells who sheltered them, and he then assisted the inhabitants."

At the time of the disaster and immediately afterwards, those involved would have thought only of offering help. But it was still bitterly cold and the waterways had clearly been frozen solid, as the foot-thick blocks of ice left on the road suggest. The policeman had fallen in at one stage and must have been soaking wet and cold in his heavy uniform. Would there have been time for him to rush home to Running Horse Yard and change into dry clothes in order to continue his work, or was it he to bear a long night of arduous work, fuelled by adrenalin and with little time to feel the extreme discomfort?

This report reveals a second hero, the butcher, Mr Plim. The Plims can also be found in the Census in 1841. Their shop and home was near the Market Place. Martin Plim was 52, his wife Lucy 55 and their son Martin 24. Was it the father or the son who went out to help, or possibly both? Someone with enough presence of mind to take a bullock rope might suggest the older man was involved in this rescue, but the great strength need to haul a woman up the side of the bridge might point to the son.

A number of other courageous actions and heroic efforts were to be reported in *The Times* over the days following the flood.

Beside the canal was a tan-yard where leather was processed in large brick lined pits[5]. Its warehouses were stocked with oak bark ready for future use in the tanning process, the whole of which was carried away by the flood water and deposited across Brentford High Street. Mr. and Mrs. Birch, described as "having the care of the premises", were awoken from their sleep when water got into their bed. They only had a short time to jump out and then, climbing onto some outbuildings, got onto the wall at the rear of the premises of their neighbour, Mr Matthews, a cooper or barrel-maker. He was awakened by their screams for help, found a ladder and got them down safely.

On Sunday morning it was feared that the crews of the wrecked boats must all have drowned - it took some hours before stories of their escapes became known. The Tolleys, a family with seven children, had been on board a canal boat belonging to Price & Sons of Brierley Hill which had been sunk. However, the Ayres family, who lived in a cottage at the bottom of Boar's

---

[5] Some of these were revealed in the archaeological excavations carried out in the summer of 2001 prior to the development of the site for waterside housing.

the Ayres family…managed to rescue all of the children by dragging them in through a window as the boat passed by

Head Yard, had managed to rescue all of the children by dragging them in through a window as the boat passed by! The reporter visited them and heard that the parents had also been saved. At the next cottage were two sisters named Forster, each with one child, who had similarly been rescued from another boat.

A further twenty-one men, women and children from the canal boats had managed to clamber over the wall of Syon House grounds as they passed and were found sheltering in a cow-house by the Duke's gardener. The first to get over, a boy named John Jones, had fastened a rope to a tree by means of which he helped the others over. As they did so, the wall gave way beneath them. Fortunately

it fell towards the grounds rather than into the water and the last boy was thrown to safety on dry land. The report emphasised their heartfelt gratitude for the shelter and succour provided by his Grace's gardener, and this was to become a refrain in all the future reports of those who had been rescued.

a boy named John Jones, had fastened a rope to a tree by means of which he helped the others over. As they did so, the wall (of Syon Park) gave way beneath them

Crowds flock to Brentford

In the immediate aftermath of the flood Brentford people were either dealing with their own problems or supporting others who were very likely to have lost everything overnight. Nevertheless they were to prove extremely resourceful and enterprising in dealing with the crowds who appeared to see

...numbers of persons have, during the day, been conveyed by boat at one halfpenny each ... for the purpose of having a nearer view of that scene of destruction which baffles all description

the scene of the disaster. The report on 18 January only mentioned that the town was "crowded with persons from all the neighbouring parts" – it is possible that some of them had come to offer help. By the next day, however, *The Times* was reporting that "numbers of persons have, during the day, been conveyed by boat at one halfpenny each to the footbridge close to the accumulation of wrecks off Boar's Head Yard, for the purpose of having a nearer view of that scene of destruction which baffles all description".

Over the following two days the crowds increased. On 19 January it was a market day in Brentford. Reports appeared on the following day, that "persons of every grade" had come from Richmond, Kingston, Hounslow, Uxbridge and Harrow "desirous of obtaining a sight of the damage". On Wednesday, 20 January it was a particularly fine day which again encouraged crowds of sightseers – "throughout the day every avenue leading to the banks of the Grand Junction Canal, from which a view could be obtained, has been thronged by persons having that object". On 22 January *The Times* reported that

> "the interest excited in the public mind by the late calamitous overflow of the waters of the Brent, &c, appears daily on the increase and the number of persons who have throughout the day flocked into Brentford has far exceeded that on either of the previous days. Carriages filled principally with elegantly dressed ladies have been rolling into the town from all parts and numbers of their fair occupants, not satisfied with viewing the scene of devastation from the shore at the bottom of Boar's Head Yard, have trusted themselves to the safe conduct of the watermen (whose fragile barks have throughout the day been most dangerously crowded) for the sake of having a nearer view from the wooden bridge."

Another group of men also came to profit from the disaster. Dredgermen came up river from Lambeth, where normally they were employed on the

VIEW OF THE LATE CALAMITOUS
WRECK AT BRENTFORD,
Occasioned by the bursting of the Banks & Locks on the Grand Junction Canal.

ON SATURDAY NIGHT THE 16th JAN.y 1841.

The lithograph of the wrecked boats beside the wall of the Duke of Northumberland's estate.

extremely arduous work of dredging the river to keep the Pool of London clear for shipping. Their equipment enabled them to fish up sacks of grain and other freight from the sunken vessels for which they were charging one shilling for every sack lifted. It appeared that this was so profitable that they began also to remove sacks from within the vessels as well as collecting those which had been thrown clear – and the boat owners saw their cargoes, however badly damaged, disappearing.

The report mentioned that an artist had been taking sketches of the scene and that lithographs were to be produced for sale. If this were done quickly it would have found a ready market amongst the sightseers. Copies of the print of the piled up wrecks are to be found in the collections of the National Waterways Museum and in Hounslow's Local Studies Collection so this part of the report can be validated[6]. The print is grandly entitled "View of the Late Calamitous Wreck at Brentford Occasioned by the bursting of the Banks and Locks on the Grand Junction Canal" and was "Drawn, Lithographed & Published" on 23 January by E Wildman.

---

[6] A large water-colour sketch of a similar view has recently been acquired for the Local Studies Collection and both a folded copy of the print and a small watercolour sketch of the same view have been bound with many other illustrations into one of its copies of Faulkner's *History & Antiquities of Brentford, Ealing and Chiswick* published in 1845. Both of these appear to *follow* the print rather than being preliminary sketches. Indeed the small sketch is dated incorrectly 1840, suggesting that it was not contemporary.

Helping those in need

Many of those who had survived the most serious flooding were made homeless, at least temporarily. This affected about 50 households whose cottages were under water and about 70 people whose boats, on which they had lived and worked, were damaged or lost. Their situation was already serious. The very severe weather of the previous five weeks had meant that not only were the boatmen and their families stranded, with their boats trapped in the ice, but many local people could not work and were also in difficulty. With no income, the boatmen in particular had been reduced to begging in the town.

With no income, the boatmen in particular had been reduced to begging in the town.

The inhabitants of Brentford had already raised a subscription to pay for necessities for those in difficulties because of the weather, but they had now virtually spent it. Covering the cost of this new emergency was going to be difficult. Writing in the 18 January edition of *The Times* the reporter explained the parish's financial problems and said "it is hoped that charitably disposed persons in other places will contribute…and we are authorised to say that anything forwarded to the vicar and churchwardens will be most thankfully received".

On the first afternoon after the Flood, three of the Guardians of the local Poor Law Union (which ran the workhouse), Messrs Hazard, Grainger and Layton, visited the poorest people whose houses had been damaged and offered them emergency relief. Workshops, businesses and homes needed to be dried out and cleaned up as quickly as possible. The fifty or so poor cottages between the High Street and the river which had been flooded were quickly provided with one and a half hundredweight of coal each, to help with drying out these properties; later each received a further two hundredweight to continue this slow task.

Ninety of the boat people were soon housed in two rooms of the National Infants' School at the south-east corner of the Butts. Though the home of the Vicar, Dr Stoddart, was described as being "partly under water" he "strenuously exerted himself in assisting all who needed it" especially supporting the boatmen's families at the Infants' School. John Stoddart, Doctor of Divinity, is listed in the 1841 Census, aged 45, with his wife Amy and four children, of which his eldest son was a surgeon, and three servants. He must have left his family and servants to dry out his home.

The *Times* reporter provides the details of the care offered to the boat people. On the 18th Dr Stoddart, with Mr Bunting and Mr Hopkins, the Churchwardens, had organised coffee, bread and butter for them at 6pm. The sixty who could not return to their boats were each provided with a supper of half a pound of beef, half a pound of bread and a pint of beer at 9pm. An hour later, straw was laid out for them to sleep on. By 8 o'clock the following morning, when a breakfast of coffee, bread and butter was provided, their number had risen to sixty-eight. On the 21st there were seventy.

The *Times* report on 20 January mentioned that the parish was aided "by the trifling subscriptions that have come in" and added, more fiercely, "it is to be regretted that a paragraph appeared in one of the papers of this morning in which are inserted the names of parties who are therein alleged to have subscribed to the extent of £500 for the relief of the boatmen, which paragraph is totally devoid of the truth, the sole subscriptions yet received not amounting to £25."

On 22 January it was reported that the boatmen and their families had also become a "sight" to visit. The *Times* of 22 January commented that "their rude manners and provincial dialect afford much amusement to their visitors". But amongst the visitors were Mr James Foster of Stourbridge, High Sheriff of Worcestershire, Mr Fryer of Bloxwich, Staffordshire and "some other gentlemen connected with the traffic on the canals". Mr Foster "delivered to them a suitable address and, on leaving, left in the hands of the Rev Dr Stoddart £10 and Mr Fryer £5" towards "the relief of these unfortunate and destitute individuals".

The presence of so many boatmen and their families underlines how busy the canal and river trade was in Brentford. Furthermore the list of tradesmen affected by the Flood and mentioned in the newspaper shows the great variety of shops and services in the town. Until funds could be raised it was not clear how they could all be compensated and Dr Stoddart's attempts to raise funds were not proving very successful. On 26 January *The Times* reported on a meeting held in the large room of the Castle Tavern the previous evening. It was attended by the most influential inhabitants of the town and neighbourhood "for the purpose of remunerating the owners of crafts and of their cargoes who have suffered from the dreadful late inundation".

Colonel Clitherow of Boston Manor House chaired the meeting and Mr Powell opened the proceedings, acknowledging the existing fund as having "a very proper object". He said, however, that "there were others who had a claim on public sympathy and liberality" by which he meant the owners of the craft and the cargoes, amongst whom were men "to whom the occurrence would bring almost absolute ruin". He proposed a motion to establish a committee and open subscriptions books at all the London and provincial banks.

Dr Stoddart was upset by this and objected. He emphasised that the priority was support for the boatmen, their wives and their families, and for the poorer inhabitants of his parish. Mr Powell's response was that he sought a separate fund, and he stressed the fact that though the owners had been wealthier than some of Brentford's poor, they had equally lost everything in some cases. The notion of a separate fund placated Dr Stoddart and he promptly seconded the motion. Messrs Clitherow, Jupp, Cudland, Brown and others also addressed the meeting and the motion was carried unanimously.

The committee, to be chaired by Colonel Clitherow, tactfully included Dr Stoddart and the two Churchwardens, Bunting and Hopkins. The other members of the committee, primarily local businessmen, were Sir Felix Booth (of the Brentford distillery), Mr Powell[7], Mr John Farnell (of the Isleworth brewery), Mr Hazard (John Hazard & Co ran the brewery in Old Brentford), Mr Pownall[8], Mr Jupp (the leading maltster in the town), Mr Grainger, Mr Parsons (agent to the Duke of Northumberland), Mr Cudland, Mr C Stanborough (a mill-owner in Isleworth) and Messrs Rowe (owners of the soap works). Mr Hazard was made treasurer and Mr Cudland secretary.

Information about the donations made to these funds comes first from the press. *The Times* of 22 January includes in its list (given on the next page) some who do not appear in the later published accounts. The newspaper stressed that the donations had gone to support some of the small cottagers of Brentford who had lost a good deal in the flood, as well as to the boatmen and their families.

---

[7] A Mr George Powell is listed amongst the "Gentry and Clergy" in Pigot's 1839 directory, living in Boston Road, Old Brentford. This may be the same man described as an omnibus proprietor and owner of six cottages in the yard behind the Three Pigeons, listed amongst those who had suffered losses in The Times of 19 January 1841.

[8] A member of the family who lived at Spring Grove, Isleworth, who was at this time not only a Brentford magistrate but also chairman of the Middlesex Magistrates.

Colonel, Mrs & Miss Clitherow	£25	Dr Hume, Hanwell	£10
Rev Dr Walmesley, Hanwell	£10	Mr J W Birch, Harley Street	£5
Lady Carr, Ealing	£5	Mr G A Crowder, Pall Mall E	£5
Rev J Glossop[9], Isleworth	£2	Mrs. Birch	£1
Mr Henry Pownall, Spring Grove	£5	Major Harriott, Old Cavendish St	£3
Hon St John Methuen	£3	Mr George Foster, Moorgate St. City	£10
Rev Dr Stoddart	£2	Mr T Smith, Old Brentford	£3
Earl & Countess of Denbigh	£3	Sir Felix Booth	£10
Mrs. White, Acton	£5	Miss Smith	£5
Rev J Smith, Ealing	£3.3s	Miss Booth	£1
Mr John Hazard	£5	Mr T Hope, Seymour St, Portman Sq	£5
Mr George Wood, Hanger Hill	£2	Mr J H Sich, Chiswick	£3
Messrs Joseph Dowson & Co	£5		

More detail is provided in two printed documents preserved in the Local Studies Collection at Chiswick Library. The first was issued on 3 February and is entitled **Sufferers from the Flood at New Brentford, January 17 1941**. It announces the gratitude of the Vicar and Churchwardens on behalf of all those who suffered for the donations received from the Queen and "the Nobility, Clergy, gentry and others" and includes a short statement of accounts. At this stage a total of £721.9s.6d (£721.45p) had been received and of this £483.4s.1½d (£483.21p) had been spent. Of this, £200 had been allocated to Colonel Clitherow's Committee for the relief of the owners of damaged or destroyed property, and the rest to boatmen and their families and the poor of Brentford for whom Dr Stoddart had first issued his appeal for help.

The second was issued on 26 February, again by the Vicar and Churchwardens of New Brentford, and gave a list of the subscribers' names arranged by parish, together with details of the expenditure. It assured them, from the Queen herself to the humblest servant able to offer half a crown (12½p), that "such a manifestation of pure Christian feeling and unsolicited liberality, will never be forgotten". Many are listed by name, including some local people, but others are anonymous, and appear as "a Stranger", "an Eye Witness", "a little boy" or simply with their initials. The

[9] There is a memorial to Rev Glossop, the Vicar of All Saints, on the corner of South Street in Isleworth.

SUFFERERS
FLOOD AT NE
JANUAR

The Rev. DR. STODDART, the Vic
the Churchwardens, are anxious to embra
sincere and grateful thanks to

HER MOST GRACIOUS

the QUEEN DOWAGER, the *Nobility, C*
and liberal Contributions in behalf of the S
trust, that the following Statement of the
the ample Funds they have received, wil
enabled them to relieve the 'Poor and Ne

Receipts.	£.	s.	d.
Amount of Subscriptions	721	9	6
	483	4	1½
Balance in hand .	£238	5	4½

JOH
WIL
THO

☞ *A General List of the Subscribers, together with*
hereafter be printed.

FEBRUARY 3, 1841.

FROM THE
BRENTFORD,
17, 1841.

, and Messrs. **BUNTING & HOPKINS,**
the earliest opportunity of returning their

MAJESTY THE QUEEN,

gy, Gentry, and others, for their voluntary
ferers from the above Calamity; and they
Expenditure to the present period, out of
e satisfactory to all who have so kindly
y' in the hour of great Trial and Distress.

Disbursements.	£.	s.	d.
To Boatmen and their Families, the Poor of New Brentford, and others . .	283	4	1½
To the Committee, towards the Funds for relieving the Owners of Property damaged and destroyed	200	0	0
	£483	4	1½

STODDART, D. D. Vicar.

AM BUNTING,
AS HOPKINS, } Churchwardens.

account of the Expenditure of the above Balance, will

[C. J. Murphy, Printer, New Brentford.

largest gift of £50 was from the Duke of Northumberland of Syon Park, more than twice the Queen's subscription of £21. Other donors included Baroness Rothschild of Gunnersbury who gave £10 and the Plims, Mr Plim giving 10 shillings (50p), Mrs. Plim and Mr Plim Junior giving 5 shillings each.

Mr Faulkner, described as "Author of *The History of Hammersmith*" and probably working at that time on his *History of Brentford, Ealing and Chiswick*, published in 1845, is listed as having made a donation of "80 half-quartern[10] loaves, coffee, etc". A total of £34.17s.7½d (£34.87p) was spent on expenses incurred in caring for the homeless boat people in the Infant Schools, towards which Mr Faulkner's donation must have contributed. The families from 24 narrow boats were given £83.10s in total towards their loss of property and the crews of 15 barges received £34. One of the most touching entries amongst the disbursements is the sum of £5 given to "Robert Spruce, Farrier of Old Brentford, towards the funeral expenses of his son who was drowned on 17 January". The final total raised was £813.17s (£813.85p).

The details of expenditure from the fund show that fifty-eight local businesses received compensation ranging from ten shillings (50p) to £20. Help was also given to Mr Hopkins, a portion of whose "back premises was forced down" and Mr Woods, the leather seller and currier, "whose loss is extensive". Damage to Norris' tannery was estimated at £1,000, an indication of the size of this substantial and long-established business.

Additional small sums went to G Brown (£5), Mrs Coleshill & Son (£2.10s), Mrs Ayres (£2.10s) – possibly from the family of that name from Boar's Head Yard, who had rescued the Tolleys from their barge – Miss E Vennell (£3) and Mrs Hindman (£1).

[10] A quartern loaf was made with a quartern of flour, weighing four pounds. These therefore weighed 2lbs.

Mr. Leader

RELIEF OF THE SUFFERERS

BY

THE LATE FLOOD.

NEW BRENTFORD, MIDDLESEX.

SUNDAY, JANUARY 17, 1841.

P. & M. A. Norbury, Printers, Brentford.

THE LATE FLOOD.

NEW BRENTFORD, MIDDLESEX.

JANUARY 17, 1841.

The Rev. Dr. STODDART, the Vicar, and Messrs. BUNTING and HOPKINS, the Churchwardens, take an early opportunity of laying before the Subscribers a Statement of the Funds which have been entrusted to their care in behalf of the Sufferers from the above Calamity, as well as the manner in which those Funds have been disposed of; and they sincerely hope that all, who have so kindly supplied them with the means of alleviating the general Distress, will not be less gratified with this Statement than they themselves have been in the distribution of their bounty.

In the name of the above Sufferers, Dr. STODDART and the Churchwardens have now only to offer their most dutiful acknowledgments and warmest thanks to her Most Gracious Majesty the QUEEN, the QUEEN DOWAGER, his Majesty the KING of HANOVER, his Royal Highness the DUKE of CAMBRIDGE, and other noble and benevolent Individuals, who have afforded to the "Poor and Needy," in the time of trouble *such* important and seasonable aid.

Dr. STODDART and the Churchwardens can also assure the above Royal and Noble Personages and the Subscribers in general, that such a manifestation of pure Christian feeling and unsolicited liberality will never be forgotten, either by themselves, who have had the honour of dispensing their bounty, or by the numerous Individuals in this Parish and others who partook of it; and they have the greatest pleasure in being able to add, that from *all*, words of real thankfulness, and in many cases amongst the Boatmen, the Bargemen, their Families, and the extreme Poor, even tears were not wanting to express their heartfelt gratitude for the prompt and charitable Relief which was thus afforded them.

Vicarage, New Brentford,
Feb. 26, 1841.

LIST OF SUBSCRIBERS.

	£.	s.	d.
Her Most Gracious Majesty the QUEEN	21	0	0

His Royal Highness the DUKE of CAMBRIDGE . . . 10 0 0
The ARCHBISHOP of CANTERBURY . . . 10 0 0
The DUKE of NORTHUMBERLAND . . . 50 0 0
The DUKE of CLEVELAND . . . 20 0 0
The DUCHESS DOWAGER of MONTROSE . . . 5 0 0

	£	s.	d.
Sidmouth, Lord and Lady } Addington, The Hon. Miss }	25	0	0
Denbigh, Lord and Lady, and Family	3	0	0
Morton, Lady Emily	1	0	0
Langston, Lady Julia	3	0	0
Ashbrook, Viscountess	5	0	0
Arden, Lady	5	0	0
Perceval, Lady	5	0	0
Pulteney, Lady	3	0	0
Methuen, The Hon. St. John,	3	0	0
Burdett, Sir Francis	5	0	0
Gibbons, Sir John	1	0	0
Hunter, Sir Claude	1	0	0
Scott, Sir G.	2	2	0
Wood, Colonel T. M.P.	5	0	0
Wood, Lieutenant-Colonel, M.P.	5	0	0
Patteson, Mr. Justice	5	0	0
Clitherow, Mrs. (London)	5	0	0
Paul, Snow, Esq.	5	0	0
Radfearn, Mrs. (by Lord Teign-mouth)	12	10	0
Foster, Jas. Esq. (High Sheriff of Worcestershire)	10	0	0
Fryer, —— Esq. (Bloxwich)	5	0	0
Anonymous	20	0	0
Hardwick, J. Esq.	2	0	0
A Lady	5	0	0
Willshire, Mrs.	1	0	0
Harley, Miss	5	0	0
Dennis, Mrs.	5	0	0
Greene, Rev. Cecil	0	10	0
Howard, Mr. L.	1	0	0
Pallister, Mr.	0	5	0
Wolton, Mr. H.	2	2	0
A Gentleman	0	5	0
A Stranger	0	4	6
An Eye Witness	0	6	0
S. B. P.	0	10	0

	£	s.	d.
Sedgwick, Mr. Sen.	2	2	0
Sedgwick, Mr. Jun.	2	2	0
Lincoln, Mr. A.	5	0	0
Pitts, Mr. W. G.	1	10	0
M. N.	1	0	0
R. M.	0	10	0
Sankey, Mrs.	0	10	0
Daniels and Payne, Messrs.	5	0	0
Queen Dowager's Domestics.	1	1	0
Lord Denbigh's Ditto	1	16	0
Bousfield, Master	0	5	0
S. Y.	5	0	0
S. B.	1	0	0
Fagg, Mrs.	5	0	0
Lindley, Mr. T.	1	2	6
A Young Gentleman	1	0	0
L. E. R.	1	0	0
A Stranger	0	2	0
Ditto	0	2	6
Sanders, Mr.	0	5	0
Sadgrove, Mr.	0	5	0
R. G. A.	0	10	0
A. B.	2	0	0
J. R.	1	1	0
Butterton, Rev. G. A.	5	0	0
Stewart, Mr. W.	2	2	0
Anonymous	1	0	0
Atkins, Miss	0	10	0
A Mite from a Servant	0	2	6
Mrs. Belin	1	0	0
A Gentleman	1	0	0
Merryl, Mrs.	2	0	0
Bekim, Mr. W.	1	0	0
B. G.	2	2	0
G. T.	0	2	6
Halliday, Mr.	2	0	0
Freeman, Rev. W. G.	2	0	0
Anonymous	0	10	0
Ostler, J. C. Esq.	1	1	0

	£	s.	d.
Gandy, Rev. Samuel (from the Distant Relief Fund)	3	0	0
Bourchier, Colonel	1	0	0
Bourchier, Miss	3	0	0
Gordon, Rev. W.	3	0	0
Drummond, Messrs. and Co.	10	0	0
Herbst, Mrs.	5	0	0
Ward, Mr. H.	2	2	0
Crawley, John, Esq.	5	0	0
Colman, Mr.	0	10	0
Barker, Mr.	5	0	0
Birch, J. W. Esq.	5	0	0
Birch, Mrs.	1	0	0
Mitchell, Mr.	1	0	0
Lindo, D. A. Esq.	10	0	0
Foster, G. Esq.	1	0	0
Willshire, J. Esq.	1	0	0
Crowder, G. A. Esq.	5	0	0
Fletcher, Mr. Joseph	1	0	0
Hope, Rev. F. W.	5	0	0
A Lady	0	10	0
M'Kenzie, Mr.	1	0	0
Walker, Mr. G.	1	0	0
Hawker, J. Esq.	1	0	0
Ward, Rev. R.	1	0	0
Cutto, A. W. Esq.	2	2	0
Rivington, Mr. J.	0	10	0
Hotham, W. Esq.	1	0	0
Talbot, Mr. James	0	5	0
A little Boy	0	0	6
Baker, Mr.	0	1	0
Bird, Mr.	0	2	0
R. E.	1	0	0
Stone, Mr. G.	5	0	0
Stone, Mr. J.	0	10	0
Hope, John Thomas, Esq.	2	0	0
Strahan, W. Esq.	15	0	0
Reeves, Miss	5	1	0
Reeves, Mr. James	1	1	0

LIST OF SUBSCRIBERS.

	£	s.	d.
A Servant	0	2	6
A Lady	0	10	0
Lieutenant-General M.	1	0	0
Weaver, Mr. and Friend	0	10	0
Hickson, Mr.	1	0	0
C. A. T.	2	0	0
C. A. Z.	1	0	0
Two Ladies	0	15	0
Stewart, James, Esq.	5	0	0
Smith, Mrs. H.	1	0	0
Wales, Mr.	1	0	0
Garven, Mrs.	2	0	0
Ronalds, Dr.	5	0	0
Miner, John, Esq.	3	0	0
Harrod, Mr.	0	1	6
Taylor, Mr. George	0	1	0
Williams, Mr. Thomas	0	1	0
A Friend	0	2	6
Laxton, Mr.	1	0	0
	£37	**18**	**6**

Faulkner, Mr. (Author of *The History of Hammersmith*), a Donation of 80 Half-quartern Loaves, Coffee, &c.

ACTON.

	£	s.	d.
Antrobus, Rev. W.	5	0	0
Wegg, Miss	30	0	0
White, Mrs. and Hatsell, Miss }	5	0	0
Winter, ——, Esq.	1	0	0
	£41	**0**	**0**

NEW BRENTFORD.

	£	s.	d.
Annand, Mr.	0	10	0
Banks, Rev. M.	1	0	0
Barnes, Mrs.	0	5	0
Barnes, Miss	0	10	0

	£	s.	d.
Norbury, Messrs.	0	5	0
Left at Ditto by a Gentleman	0	1	0
Oliver, Captain	1	1	0
Palmer, Mr.	0	2	6
Pearce, Mrs.	0	2	6
Pearce, Mrs. (Red Lion)	0	5	0
Pitt, Miss	1	0	0
Plim, Mr.	0	10	0
Plim, Mrs.	0	5	0
Plim, Mr. Jun.	0	5	0
Powell, Miss	0	8	0
Priest, Miss	0	10	0
Racketts, Mr.	0	5	0
Radcliff, Mr.	0	5	0
Rattliff, Mrs.	0	2	6
Rattliff, Miss	0	2	6
Reynolds, Miss	0	10	0
Robinson, Mrs.	1	0	0
Ronalds, Mr. J.	0	10	0
Sanders, Mr. W.	0	2	6
Saxton, Mr.	0	10	0
Sexton, Messrs.	1	0	0
Shury, Mrs.	0	2	6
Simpson, Mr.	0	2	6
Smallwood, Mr.	0	10	0
Squire, Mr.	0	2	6
Stephenson, Mr. G. J.	0	5	0
Stoddart, Rev. Dr.	1	0	0
Stoddart, Mrs.	0	5	0
Swapp, Mr.	0	2	6
Thorn, Mr.	0	2	6
Thwaites, Miss	0	2	6
Tillyer, Mr.	1	0	0
Tinson, Mr.	0	2	6
Tomson, Captain	1	0	0
Trimmer, Miss (Butts)	0	2	6
Upjohn, Mr.	0	2	6
Walbran, Mr.	0	5	0
Walbran, Miss	0	2	6
Walkling, Mr.	0	2	6
Waters, Mr.	0	10	0
Wheatley, Mrs.	0	2	6
Whitman, Mr.	0	5	0

	£	s.	d.
Farmer, Thomas, Esq.	2	0	0
F. Mr. (Friend of)	0	10	0
Fisher, Mrs. Jedderey	2	0	0
Furber, Mrs.	1	10	0
Hopgood, Mr.	1	0	0
Rothschild, Baroness	10	0	0
Sleap, Mr. J. T.	0	10	0
Smith, Rev. John	2	2	0
Smith, Miss	1	1	0
Stephenson, Mrs.	0	10	0
Willis, Mr. F.	5	0	0
Wood, Mr. G.	2	0	0
S. T. G. (by Mr. Mott, of Gunnersbury)	5	0	0
	£40	**8**	**0**

GREENFORD.

	£	s.	d.
Tomkins, Rev. Mr.	0	10	0
	£0	**10**	**0**

HANWELL.

	£	s.	d.
Goring, Mr. H.	0	2	6
Hume, Dr.	20	0	0
Rochfort, Mrs.	0	5	0
Swayne, Mr.	0	2	0
Walmsley, Rev. Dr.	5	0	0
	£25	**9**	**6**

HARLINGTON.

	£	s.	d.
Brown, Mr.	1	1	0
	£1	**1**	**0**

HOUNSLOW.

	£	s.	d.
Camden, Mr. G. J.	1	0	0
Pownall, H. Esq.	5	0	0
Smythe, Mrs.	1	0	0

OLD BRENTFORD.

	£	s.	d.
Donations from Poor in the Butts, by Mr. Winkworth	0	5	0
Servants at Boston House	1	0	0
	£64	15	6

OLD BRENTFORD.

	£	s.	d.
Booth, Sir Felix, Bart.	10	0	0
Booth, Miss	1	0	0
Bolton, Miss	0	10	0
Clarke, Mr. J.	1	0	0
Crane, Mrs.	0	10	0
Crane, Mrs. E.	0	5	0
Evans, Mr. G.	0	10	0
Evans, Mr. J.	1	0	0
Evans, Mr. Jos.	0	10	0
Hazard, Mr. J.	5	0	0
Lyle, Mr. W. G.	2	2	0
Nicholas, Mr. A.	1	0	0
Osborne, Mr.	1	0	0
Platt, Miss	1	0	0
Richards, Mr.	0	3	0
Round, Mrs.	0	10	0
Scratchard, Miss.	5	0	0
Smith, Mr. Thomas	5	0	0
Smith, Miss	1	0	0
Trimmer, Miss	0	10	0
Trimmer, Miss S.	1	0	0
Yonge, Rev. W. C.	1	0	0
	£39	10	0

CHISWICK.

	£	s.	d.
Dickinson, Mr. (Kew Bridge)	1	0	0
D. Mr. (Two Ladies, Friends of)	1	5	0
Sich, Mr. J. H.	3	0	0
Williams, Captain	1	0	0
	£6	5	0

EALING.

	£	s.	d.
Atkinson, Mr.	1	0	0
Batty, Mr.	0	5	0
Butler, Mr. John	1	0	0
Carr, Lady	5	0	0

	£	s.	d.
Beck, Mr.	0	5	0
Blake, Mr.	0	2	6
Blyth, Miss	0	7	0
Brooks, Mr.	0	10	0
Cooper, Dowager Lady	2	0	0
Day, Mr. W.	2	0	0
Dowson, Messrs.	5	5	0
Glossop, Rev. H.	3	3	0
Gordon, Lord and Lady	2	0	0
Hodgson, Miss	1	0	0
Honeywood, W. Esq.	0	10	0
Miss Lane's School	0	10	0
Parsons, Mr.	1	0	0
Pepper, Mr.	0	10	0
Warren, Mr.	0	10	0
E. K.	0	10	0
	£20	7	6

KENSINGTON.

	£	s.	d.
Haynes, Mr.	0	5	0
Philp, Dr.	0	10	0
Searle, Mr.	5	0	0
Webster, Mr. J.	0	10	0
	£6	5	0

KEW.

	£	s.	d.
Byam, Rev. Burgh	2	0	0
Carey, Miss	0	10	0
M'Donald, Mrs.	0	10	0
Selwyn, Mr. W.	5	0	0
Scheer, Mr.	2	0	0
Schnell, Mrs.	0	10	0
Tyrrell, Mrs.	2	0	0
Wylde, Miss	2	0	0
	£14	10	0

KNIGHTSBRIDGE.

	£	s.	d.
Ashe, Rev. J. P.	2	2	6
De Bois, Madame de Chevaline	1	1	0
Gordon, Miss	1	1	0
	£4	4	6

	£	s.	d.
Brown, Miss (a Friend, by)	0	10	0
Bunting, Mr.	0	10	0
Carrington, Mrs.	0	5	0
Cherry, Mr.	1	0	0
Christmas, Mrs.	0	2	6
Clark, Mr. J.	0	10	0
Clarke, Mr. G. (Butts)	0	10	0
Clitherow, Colonel	10	0	0
Clitherow, Mrs.	10	0	0
Clitherow, Miss	5	0	0
Coombs, Mr.	0	2	6
Coombs, Mrs.	0	2	6
Combaz, Mr.	0	2	6
Cooper, Mr. G.	1	0	0
Collett, Mr.	0	2	6
Collett, Miss	0	2	6
Crighton, Mr.	0	5	0
Curnock, Mrs.	0	5	0
Cullen, Mr.	0	10	0
Darnell, Mrs.	0	5	0
Dewell, Mrs.	0	10	0
Dexter, Mr.	0	5	0
Ellis, Mr.	0	2	6
Fletcher, Mr. R.	0	1	0
Fletcher, Mrs. Major	1	0	0
Flower, Mr.	0	10	0
Franklin, Mrs.	0	2	6
Glover, Mr. Sen.	1	1	0
Glover, Mr. Jun.	1	1	0
Goring, Mr.	0	5	0
Grocock, Mr.	0	5	0
Hammond, Mr.	0	5	0
Haynes, Mr.	0	2	6
Hearn, Miss	0	5	0
Hill, Mr.	0	2	6
Hinge, Mr. J.	0	2	6
Hodgson, Mrs.	0	5	0
Hopkins, Mr.	0	10	0
Jones, Mr.	0	2	6
Kayes, Mr.	0	10	0
King, Mr.	0	2	6
Lanchester, Mrs.	0	2	6
Leader, Mr.	0	5	0
Lewis, Mrs.	2	0	0
Mansell, Miss	0	1	0
Moore, Mrs.	0	2	6
Murphy, Mr.	0	2	6

LIST OF SUBSCRIBERS.

MORTLAKE.

	£.	s.	d.
Aynscombe, Mrs.	5	0	0
King, Mr and Son	0	4	0
K. Mr. (Friends of)	0	3	0
Ommaney, Rev. E. H.	0	10	0
Pattison, Rev. Mr. (a Friend of Mr. Ommaney)	0	10	0
Unknown	0	10	0
C. B.	0	10	0
C. V.	2	0	0
	£7	17	0

RICHMOND.

Blyth, Dr.	0	3	0
Ellis, Mrs.	0	2	6
Macclesfield, Countess of	5	5	0
Penrhyn, E. Esq. (East Sheen),	2	0	0

	£.	s.	d.
Price, Sir Charles, Bart. (Spring Grove)	1	1	0
Selwyn, Mrs. E.	1	0	0
Shaw, Mrs.	0	10	0
Twining, J. Esq. (East Sheen),	1	0	0
Twining, R. G. Esq.	0	5	0
A Friend	1	0	0
W. A.	0	5	0
C. B.	0	2	6
I. C. M.	0	1	0
Sundry Subscriptions	0	13	6
	£14	7	6

TEDDINGTON.

Ronalds, Mrs. Hugh	1	0	0
	£1	0	0

TWICKENHAM.

	£.	s.	d.
Burt, Rev. R.	1	0	0
Beauchamp, Miss	3	0	0
Cambridge, The Ven. Archdeacon,	5	0	0
Cambridge, C. O. Esq.	5	0	0
Gimingham, Mr.	0	10	6
Gimingham, Mrs.	3	0	0
Harriott, Major	0	10	0
Hodges, Mrs.	0	2	6
Ives, Mr. Jun.	2	0	0
Maclew, Mr.	2	0	0
Peel, Colonel	0	5	0
Staples, Mrs.	0	10	0
Stephenson, Miss	0	10	0
Tubbs, Miss			
	£24	8	0

BALANCE SHEET.

RECEIPTS.

	£.	s.	d.
Her Most Gracious Majesty the QUEEN	21	0	0
The QUEEN DOWAGER	20	0	0
His Majesty the KING of HANOVER	21	0	0
His Royal Highness the DUKE of CAMBRIDGE	10	0	0
The ARCHBISHOP of CANTERBURY	10	0	0
The DUKE of NORTHUMBERLAND	50	0	0
The DUKE of CLEVELAND	20	0	0
The DUCHESS DOWAGER of MONTROSE	5	0	0
London, &c.	337	18	6
The Parish of Acton	41	0	0
New Brentford	64	15	6
Old Brentford	39	10	0
Chiswick	6	5	0

DISBURSEMENTS.

	£.	s.	d.
To the *Boatmen* and their Families, belonging to 24 Boats, towards their Loss of Property	83	10	0
To the *Relief afforded to the above Persons*, at the Infant School Room, during 11 Days, and Expenses incurred there	34	17	7½
To the *Crews* of 15 *Barges*, towards their Loss of Property	34	0	0
To the *Poor Families* of New Brentford, who suffered from the Flood, Coals, Bread, &c. and Money, in Sums varying from 10s. to £3.	154	6	1½
To *Tradesmen* and *others* of New Brentford, whose Property was much damaged or destroyed; viz.:			

	£.	s.	d.		£.	s.	d.
Mr. Trimmer	20	0	0	Miss E. Vennell	3	0	0

	£	s	d
Hanwell	25	9	6
Harlington	1	1	0
Hounslow	7	0	0
Isleworth	20	7	6
Kensington	6	5	0
Kew	14	10	0
Knightsbridge	4	4	6
Mortlake	7	17	0
Richmond	14	7	6
Teddington	1	0	0
Twickenham	24	8	0

£813 17 0

	£	s	d
Coates			
Marsden	1	10	0
Yeaxley	10	0	0
Thorn	10	0	0
Eustance	1	5	0
Heap	7	0	0
A. Harris	1	10	0
Tinson	7	0	0
Gray	2	10	0
Brasher	7	0	0
Plim	2	0	0
Clark	5	5	0
Norminton	1	10	0
Best	5	5	0
Harris	1	0	0
G. Brown	5	0	0
H. Brown	1	0	0
Cook	5	0	0
Marden	1	0	0
Matthews	4	0	0
Miss Heath	1	0	0
Whitehorn	3	0	0
Mr. Racketts	1	0	0
Mrs. Coleshill & Son	2	10	0
Mrs. Hindman	1	0	0
Ayres	2	10	0
Mr. Carver	0	15	0
Mr. Ferguson	3	0	0
Sweet	0	10	0

158 15 0

To the following Owners of Craft and other Property, damaged or destroyed:—

	£	s	d
Mr. Charles Sims, New Brentford	£25	0	0
Townsend, Ditto	20	0	0
Winter, Old Brentford	25	0	0
Skeeles, North Hyde	25	0	0
	95	0	0

To Robert Spruce, Farrier, of Old Brentford, towards the Funeral Expenses, &c. of his Son, who was drowned on the 17th of January — 5 0 0

To the Police Force of the T Division, under Inspector Marquard, by whose prompt exertions much Property and in all probability many Lives were saved, 10 0 0

To Messengers, the delivery of Circulars, posting of Bills, postage of Letters, Parcels, &c. — 4 12 3

To Messrs. Norbury and Mr. Murphy, for Printing and Stationery — 11 11 0

To the *Inundation Committee*, towards those Owners of Craft, &c. who most require Assistance — 200 0 0

To Ditto, additional, received by Dr. Stoddart — 22 5 0

£813 17 0

JOHN STODDART, D. D. Vicar.
WILLIAM BUNTING, } Churchwardens.
THOMAS HOPKINS,

VICARAGE, NEW BRENTFORD,
February 26th, 1841.

Victims of the Flood

Information from *The Times* 19 January, Pigot's Middlesex Directory 1839 and disaster fund accounts

South side of High Street

Name	Description	Sum paid
Mr Trimmer	Black Boy Inn	£20
Mr Piper	Six Bells *"in whose cellar the liquor casks burst"*	£10
Mr Ware	Beer shop	£10
Mr Hatton	Hair cutter	£2.10s
Mr Eustance	Pork butcher	£1.5s
Mr Gray	Tinman or whitesmith	£2.10s
Mr Plim	Butcher	£2
Mr Norminton	Dyer	£1.10s
Mr H Harris	Shopkeeper and general dealer	£1
Mr Boxall	Pastrycook	
Mr Lindley	Fruiterer	
Mrs Whitman		
Mr Curtis	Corn and coal merchant	
Mr Lowe	Tailor	
Mrs Hearn	Dressmaker	
Mr H Brown	Fruiterer, greengrocer	£1
Mr Racketts	Greengrocer	£1
Mr Carver	Mutual Fire office agent	15s
Dr Stoddart	Vicarage	
Victoria Coffee House		
Mr Woods	Leatherseller & currier *"whose loss is extensive"*	

The tables show the names of the victims of flood damage assembled from the newspaper reports and other sources. Where known, their businesses are also listed, together with the amounts of compensation they were given.

North side of High Street

Name	Description	Sum paid
Mr Simmonds	Baker	£15
Mr Yeaxley	Painter, glazier, paper hanger	£10
Mr Thorn	Plumber	£10
Mr Heap	Carpenter	£7
Mr Tinson	Three Pigeons Inn	£7
Mr Brasher	Upholsterer, owned houses near bridge	£7
Mr Clark	Attorney	£5.5s
Mr Best	Grocer	£5
Mr G Brown		£5
Mr Cook	Boot and shoemaker	£5
Mr Matthews	Cooper	£4
Mr Whitehorn	Tobacconist, corner of house severely damaged by barge	£3
Mr Ferguson	Chemist	£3
Mr Woodbridge	Stationer	£2.10s
Mr Marsden	Harness-maker	£1.10s
Mr Coombs	Auctioneer	£2
Mr A Harris	Greengrocer, fruiterer	£1.10s
Miss Heath	Milliner	£1
Mr Hopkins	Salesman, *"portion of back premises forced down"*	
Mr Norris	Tanyard	
Mr Sweet	Statuary	10s
Mr Dowden	Coachmaker	
Alton Arms	Beershop	
Mr Heap	Carpenter	
Mr Farrell	Surgeon	
Mr Hearn	Hairdresser	
Mr Jones	Hosier	
Mr Powell	Omnibus proprietor, owned 6 cottages at Three Pigeons	
Mr Norris	Tanner, damage *"estimated at £1,000"*	
Messrs Clacks	Solicitors' office	
Mr Winckworth	Builder	
The Savings Bank		

Clearing the canal & recovering the cargoes

For a town so dependant upon its waterways, the clearing of the wrecks which blocked them was a high priority once those suffering immediate hardship had been found food, clothing and shelter. Furthermore, it was important for their owners to retrieve the boats and salvage their cargoes as they represented a substantial element of their livelihood. Again it is the newspaper reports which provide information about the meetings held, decisions made and actions taken. The first day of real action on this matter was Tuesday 19 January. "During the day", *The Times* reported, "several of the leading millers, maltsters and wharfingers have been in communication with the City Navigation Committee and with the directors of the Grand Junction Canal, on the subject of raising and removing the wrecks which now totally impede the navigation of the canal and thereby ascertaining the extent of the damage done."

A number of the interested parties first assembled at the Three Pigeons, the very large inn on the west side of the Market Place, at 3 o'clock but decided to adjourn the meeting until 7 o'clock that evening. Amongst those present were Mr H Hall and Messrs Grainger, Banyon, Layton, Winter, Sims, Jupp and Brown[11]. The meeting asked Mr Banyon to take the chair and he set out the purpose of calling everyone together. He said that they should "devise and adopt the best means to clear away the wrecks and thereby re-open the navigation, which he conceived to be the best thing that could be done under the melancholy circumstances".

Mr Hall was asked to report to the meeting on his visit to the City of London navigation authorities, where he had been to find out who had responsibility for the stretch of water that was obstructed. The newspaper does not give any details about Mr Hall, but a letter from Uxbridge published without a sender's name appeared in *The Times* of 22 January stating that the Mr Hall mentioned in *The Times'* reports was actually Mr Hull, an Uxbridge miller. This was the man whose corn was loaded into Fowler's barges so he certainly had a significant interest in seeing that the vessels were raised quickly.

---

[11] William Grainger of New Brentford appears in Pigot's 1839 Directory of Middlesex as a dealer in both corn and grain, as do William and Henry Jupp and Thomas Layton of Old Brentford; all three are also listed as maltsters, processing the grain. John Brown of New Brentford is listed as a carpenter and builder and a coal merchant, while Robert Banyon and Thomas Winter of Old Brentford appear as barge masters. Mr Sims is not in the Directory and could have been a relative newcomer at the time of the Flood.

"Mr Hall said, when he entered Brentford that morning and saw the deplorable state in which the craft and the property they contained had been reduced by the violence of the flood, he inquired who were the persons who had command over that portion of the stream. He at first heard that it was the City, and then that it was the Grand Junction Canal Company; and as great distress had arisen by the stoppage of the navigation, he thought it his duty to proceed to the City to see what could be done in the matter. He then learned that the City had no jurisdiction in the matter, and that the duty belonged to the Canal Company.

Common sense telling him that it was as much the interest of the Canal Company to clear the canal that the navigation might continue, as it was that of the sufferers, he consulted Mr Saunders and Mr Layton, and ultimately thought it his duty to go to the Canal Company where he was happy to say, he had been met in a most liberal manner. Mr Seale, whom he saw, could not, however, pledge himself as to what might be done, but gave him a letter to Sir Francis Head, to whom he went. Sir Francis Head immediately said, "Yes, we'll help you, and you must help us for, although the navigation belongs to the Company, the boats and freight do not." They had therefore, to settle what body of men each of the sufferers could send to assist, and Sir Francis Head would meet them at 9 o'clock tomorrow morning to settle the remainder."

The meeting assembled a list of the names of the wrecked craft with details of their cargoes and recorded to whom they belonged. They agreed that the owner of each boat should send men to assist with the work, four men for each barge and two men for each boat. They would meet up at the site of the most serious wreckage at 6 o'clock the next morning. This they did, but unfortunately they did not have the right equipment for such an enormous and complex task, nor was there anyone appropriate to take charge of it.

Sir Francis Head arrived on the scene at 9 o'clock, was told of the decision of the meeting the night before and immediately objected to it! He felt the responsibility lay with the Navigation Committee of the Thames to see to the raising of the wrecks. If they would not do it the Canal Company would, but he wanted the boat owners to agree that his officers be allowed to take charge of the whole process. After considerable discussions, they agreed to this with the aim of starting the operations the next morning. While this argument had been going on, the men assembled earlier that day had not been completely idle, having spent some time removing rigging and masts to make it easier to manoeuvre the wrecks. However, one more boat sank overnight.

The Wildman lithograph shows both Thames barges and monkey boats wrecked in the water, but there is no illustration of other damage. Though some of the canal boats were washed through Brentford Bridge, others moored just above it must have been wrecked as the arch of the bridge became blocked. The table lists nine narrow boats which had been lost and another nine which were badly damaged, with all the details we have about them.

The Thames barges seem to have fared better, and few were completely lost as a result of the flood, though the descriptions and the lithograph suggest otherwise. Five barges loaded with grain were found stacked against Mr Fowler's wharf at Brentford End, just below Brentford Bridge, and these were at first thought to be a total loss. They belonged to Charles Saunders, a lighterman of Strand on the Green and held 1800 quarters of corn and 350 quarters of linseed. 1300 quarters of the grain were the property of Hulls, the Uxbridge millers. One of the barges was soon "got up" and was described as not having been so badly damaged as had been expected, but much of the grain must have been ruined. The Susan, a barge said to belong to Mr Skeeles[12] of North Hyde, near Southall, was said to be amongst the wrecks at the bottom of Boar's Head Yard. The disaster fund accounts show that four barge owners were to receive a total of £95 compensation: Mr Charles Sims and Mr Townsend of New Brentford, Mr Winter of Old Brentford and Mr Skeeles, so their loss must have been the greatest.

The removal operations finally began on Thursday 21 January. A large group of men, supervised by Mr Lake, the Grand Junction Canal Company's clerk of works, assembled off Boar's Head Yard with cranes, grabs and other gear with which to handle the damaged and sunken vessels. Crowds again assembled to watch; The Times reporter commented that they stayed for may hours despite the extreme cold. Though very little lifting was possible that day before dusk fell, it was predicted that it might be possible to remove enough of the damaged vessels for the navigation to re-open the following Monday.

It is possible to trace some information about the barge-owners involved. Pigot's Middlesex Directory, published in 1839, lists ten barge masters and

---

12 Mentioned first as "Mr Scheel" of North Hyde in The Times' report of 18 January 1841.

Canal boats lost or damaged in the flood at Brentford
Information assembled from newspaper reports

Boats sunk or broken up and "of which no trace has yet been discovered"

Boat name	Cargoes	Owner	Place of origin
The Safety The Diligent	Coals and peas	Mr Bissell	Tipton, near Birmingham
The Julia The Kingfisher	Hoop iron	Mr Josiah Smith	Bloxwich, Staffordshire
The Tipton Lass The Adelaide	Coals	Bradley & Co	Tipton, near Birmingham
The Oak The London Trader	70 quarters wheat 24½ quarters wheat	John Bradley & Co	Stourbridge
The Ashley Company	Empty	The Ashley Company	Not known

Boats described as "seriously injured"

Boat name	Cargoes	Owner	Place of origin
The Union The John	Not known	Mr Shipton	Wolverhampton
The Amiable	Not known	Mr Walter Williams	West Bromwich
The Liberty "An iron boat not named" The Prosperous	Slate and Quarry tiles	Boats "hired by" John Dalfern, freight the property Mr Dale, Brentford	Nuneaton, Warwickshire
The Sarah The John Price	Not known	Price & Sons	Brierley Hill
The Henry	Not known	Michael Hall	Gospel Oak, Tipton, near Birmingham

"…and several others, not named, barges and lighters, to a total of about 20"

Horse-drawn barges, the monkey boats of the press reports, which worked the canals in the early 19th century (from W H Pyne's *Microcosm* 1802).

lightermen, almost all of whose names are mentioned in the reports of the flood. They were John Baker, Robert Banyon, Joseph Harris, Thomas Layton, John Napper and Thomas Winter from Old Brentford and William Bourne, Joseph Dale, Francis Rogers & Son and William George Townsend of New Brentford.

The records of the Watermen's Company in the Guildhall Library provide details of barges working on the Thames in manuscript lists of craft and their owners. William Fowler, for example, appears from around 1800 as owner number 30, with his address given as Syon Wharf, the wharf just below the Bridge. His boats, most built by Joseph Piper of Hammersmith, include a William Henry (though the press reports are confusing and mentioned both "William Henry" and "William and Henry" as the name of his boat). Matilda is the barge which he almost certainly lost in the Flood; in the list it has been crossed out with the date 30 April 1841 noted alongside.

John Saunders of Strand on the Green is listed as owner 636; Charles Saunders took over his boats in 1839. He has quite a list of craft but it is not possible to identify whether any of those later deleted from this list were lost in the Flood as the deletions are not dated. However, the list does suggest a long-standing business relationship with the Hulls, the Uxbridge millers whose grain he was transporting in 1841, as William Hull sold his barge Prudence (also built by Joseph Piper) to John Saunders in 1812.

Mr Skeele appears from 1816 as owner number 740, first at Isleworth and later at North Hyde. The Susan is not listed but if it worked the canal rather than the river it would not have been included. Thomas Winter (637), of Old Brentford owned barges Jason and Hector, which do disappear from the list though no information is provided to link them to this disaster.

Injuries, Deaths and Inquests

Besides describing the effects of the disaster on the town and on the boat families, the daily newspaper reports soon began to include details of the inquests on those who had died. These reports are invaluable as they provide the only surviving record of the proceedings. These inquests were held in one or other of Brentford's many pubs, a reminder that the main public meeting rooms were to be found in these establishments.

Charles Morris, a market gardener, went missing on the Saturday evening of the flood and his body was not discovered until Monday 18th, near his home in Brook Lane. The Times reported on the inquest into his death which opened at the White Hart in Windmill Lane on 21 January. The inquest room was very crowded and the Times reporter commented that this was because Mr Morris, "whose abilities were far above his station" had for many years been a resident in the town, "in which he was much respected."

John Henslow, Police Constable T68, gave evidence. He had met Mr Morris, who was very intoxicated, on Brentford Bridge at about 11pm on Saturday night. He was talking to a boatman, but he asked the policeman if he would see him home – he must have been aware that he was pretty drunk. The constable explained that to take him all the way home would be beyond his official beat, but offered to take him "half way down Brentford" which he did. When they reached the Half Acre Mr Morris decided very determinedly to go off on his own, though the policeman argued with him and advised him to go another way. So Morris set off alone, able to walk and not in low spirits, but without a companion – and the next the policeman heard was that he had been found drowned.

Walter Prendergast, Police Constable T79, described himself as a resident of Old Brentford, living on the premises of Colonel Lester. He knew Mr Morris and had heard he was missing on Monday morning. That afternoon, he and other constables had dragged the pond in the Colonel's grounds, which was linked to what he described as "an armlet of the Brent". First they saw a piece of cloth on the surface of the water, then they put in drags and hauled up

Charles Morris's body. He was "quite dead, and his arms were raised up with his fists clenched, as if he had been struggling hard to get out."

> his arms were raised up with his fists clenched, as if he had been struggling hard to get out

The Coroner expressed the view that he did not think Mr Morris had been violently treated despite a wound on his forehead. He had been on his way home three hours before the flood, but there was strong flowing water in the brook, seven or eight feet deep that night, and a good deal of ice being broken up by the flow. PC Prendergast thought the wound could have been made by a chunk of ice as Mr Morris fell. The jury returned a verdict of accidental death, saying there was no evidence to show how he came to be in the water.

The Times of 23 January reported that **Henry Corsell** had been found on Sunday afternoon and though severely injured, was still alive. He was in his bed in the cabin of his barge, apparently asleep but in reality insensible. He was suffering from severe concussion, his jaw had been broken in two places, and his head and chest were also badly injured. Though it was said that he had probably been "struck by the windlass" while struggling with his vessel

> He was heard to say during the height of the flood that he would save his barge or die with her

it is more likely that he was struck by the very substantial tiller which is a feature of Thames barges. He was heard to say during the height of the flood that he would save his barge or die with her; it appeared that he was likely to die but no inquest is recorded into his death.

William Fowler died in the evening of Sunday 17 January. His inquest was held at the George and Dragon at Brentford End in Isleworth Parish, close to where Mr Fowler had his business as a wharfinger and lighterman. Three of his barges had been sunk in the flood but the jury heard that his death was not felt to have been accelerated by this significant loss, because he was scarcely aware of what had happened. He was 69 and had been ailing for some years. For the last three weeks he had not left his house. On that Sunday afternoon he had left his bedroom for a short time, "when, a noise being heard, he was found in a dying state and before medical assistance could arrive, he expired." The jury returned a verdict of natural death.

The death of **William Spruce** was particularly sad because he was only about 19 years old. The finding of his body on Sunday morning was mentioned in the first detailed report from the *The Times* on 18 January. Two days later at noon the Coroner, Mr Baker, and a jury of 13 respectable householders viewed his body in the basement of the Catherine Wheel pub, went to see the wrecks at the bottom of Catherine Wheel Yard and then proceeded to receive evidence about the identity of the dead man back at the pub. Before they took any evidence, the Coroner allowed the Foreman of the Jury to report that a very strong feeling existed in the town that the disaster had in very great measure been caused by the timber floats moored in the stream. The Vicar, Dr Stoddart (who attended with all of his Churchwardens), also spoke, reporting their concern that the failure to open the lock gates had made the calamity much worse. The Coroner felt that his first responsibility was formally to identify the bodies of those who had died and later to determine the primary cause and who was liable for the damage.

The principal witness was Richard Severs, a bargeman who lived in the Ham, New Brentford. He said he had known William Spruce, a barge boy employed by Mr Fowler, and he had last seen him at about 10am on the morning of the 16th. On the Sunday morning, near the pile of wrecks which the jury had just visited, he had seen William's body lying on its side under the water. He was interrupted by a question from one of the jurors who asked "What in your opinion was the cause of the barges getting adrift?"

Mr Severs had no hesitation in saying that he believed it was the timber floats; there had been other occasions when there had been heavy floods and ice breaking up from a sudden thaw but they had not caused comparable damage. At its highest the water rose to within less than a foot of the top of the arch of Brentford bridge, which was being dammed up by the timbers. He spoke at some length about the fourteen barges and sixteen monkey-boats which had been "thrown in a heap" upwards of 20 feet above the usual level of the water, where they were still to be seen against the Duke of Northumberland's wall opposite Boar's Head Yard – this sight had clearly made a considerable impact upon him.

He explained that the heavy flow had forced away the timbers which were afloat in the Old River Brent, where they were not sufficiently well fastened, and these were then driven by the rush of water against the boats. The combination of the heavy wood as well as the fast-flowing water had torn them away to be swamped and wrecked. He felt this was an accident and could not apportion specific blame, but he said that the timber floats made the canal more dangerous to navigate. It was ascertained that the floats belonged to Messrs Dowson, Osborne and Saunders.

The Coroner started to adjourn the inquest for a week at this point, saying that a "wide and vastly important field" had been opened up for discussion which needed more time. One of the jurors requested they examine the monkey-boatmen before they adjourned, as they wanted to go to their homes as soon as that was practicable and may no longer be in Brentford when the inquest reassembled. So evidence was next heard from two of the boatmen, William Cooksey and John Jones.

William Cooksey came from Aldborough in Shropshire and was a boatman on the Queen monkey boat, the property of the Horsley Company. He described how his boat was moored outside of and attached to the barge, William Henry, which belonged to William Fowler. Between half past three and four o'clock on Sunday morning he had seen William Spruce on top of the cabin of his own barge; he had been asleep inside the cabin until they had awakened him and he had come on deck. William Cooksey had not seen William Spruce knocked off his cabin or seen him fall in but he described vigorously the scene as their boats struggled against the floodwater in the dark.

"We were coming rapidly by the force of the waters. We were going rapidly as a bird flying. The barge had both timber and ice with her...The timber kept coming down the stream for two hours and broke the barges away from their moorings. Nothing could resist the force of the timber...

We were going rapidly as a bird flying

The waters were rising for full three hours. It rose full a yard in half an hour, we were driven against the Duke of Northumberland's wall, and I put a boy over, who fastened a rope to a tree, by which means no less than twenty-one men, women and children were safely got over the wall and their lives spared...The timber floats were the cause of all the destruction, in my opinion. The river was completely blocked up by the water and ice."

John Jones came from Britannia Street in Leicester and described himself as the boat boy to the Tipton Lane monkey-boat, which belonged to Bradley & Company and had been wrecked. Earlier reports of the escape described by William Cooksey suggest that John was the boy who was put over the side of the boat to fasten a rope to a tree on the Duke's estate. His evidence was as follows:

"I knew the deceased by sight and saw him last alive about half past 3 o'clock on the morning of Sunday, standing on top of the barge William Henry belonging to Mr Fowler, his master. When I saw him he was off Mr Sim's wharf, close by where the wreck now is, and all the boats were swamped. The deceased's barge coming to a sudden stop against the Duke of Northumberland's wall, the sudden jolt and the turning of the rudder forced him off into the water. I saw no person near the deceased. I had only one sight of him in the water after he had fallen in. I did not hear him utter any cry as he fell in…

We had for two hours been engaged in guarding off the timber floats, to prevent their forcing the boats from their moorings. I attribute the whole of the mischief to the timber floats carrying away the boats and barges from their anchorage, and driving them through the bridges and by driving them in a heap damming up the waters."

I attribute the whole of the mischief to the timber floats

The Coroner remarked that the case could be one of manslaughter if it were proved that the timber floats were moored there illegally, while one of the jurors returned to the concern expressed by the vicar about the failure of the Canal Company to draw the paddles on the locks. This would have eased the flow and ensured that timber, water and ice went through safely. It is possible to imagine that the quantity of ice in the canal may have made the opening of the locks to drain off the water difficult. In the flood in 1903, for example, the canal was not frozen and the water completely overflowed the lock above Brentford Bridge, swamping the land alongside and pouring over the gates.

Subsequent days of the inquest saw counsel and solicitors attending on behalf of Spruce's relatives, Mr Fowler's executors, the owners of the timber floats and the Regent's Canal Company. The Jury and Coroner assembled at the Three Pigeons at 1 o'clock on 7 February for the fourth day of what *The Times* described as "the inquiry into the circumstances attending the death of William Spruce and the causes of the late direful inundation in the town of Brentford". The venue, in one of the largest inns in the town, was clearly chosen to accommodate a substantial audience. The room was "throughout the lengthened proceedings crowded in every part by the most influential inhabitants of the neighbourhood" – clearly concern about the true causes of the disaster, or at least the reasons for its severity, had continued to grow.

This was to be a long day. Some five hours were taken up with the matter of a witness who appeared to be refusing to give evidence. No name is given in the newspaper reports, but we are told that the witness in question had been summoned three times and had failed to appear, only now having sent a medical certificate. In fact this witness was Mr John Golden, the Regent's Canal Company's engineer, who was seriously ill. The first two hours were spent on legal argument and then there was an adjournment of three hours to allow a juror and the summoning officer to travel into London to ascertain whether Mr Golden was genuinely ill. When the inquest reconvened it was told that it would have been dangerous to the witness's health to come to Brentford and there was further discussion as to whether the proceedings should be adjourned until he was fully recovered.

Despite the fact that it was now evening, it was decided to continue. Two witnesses were questioned at great length and the proceedings did not end until 11 o'clock that night. The cross-examination related to the question of responsibility on the part of the canal authorities. Had the Grand Junction Canal Company done all it could to avert the disaster and had the Regent's Canal Company managed the flow of water from its reservoir appropriately? The substance of the evidence appeared to show that the former had done everything in its powers to prevent the disaster, though the servants of the latter had not used "proper caution" in the management of the reservoir.

A surveyor was called on behalf of the Regent's Canal Company to deal with the question of a fracture in the retaining wall or dam at the downstream end of the reservoir. He stated that "it was of a proper strength and, even much stronger than similar walls he had erected." He also said that the water which had escaped through the fracture could not have reached Brentford until nearly 5 o'clock on Sunday morning, which was after the greater part of the damage had been done. If different measures had been used for letting the water off from the reservoir, it would have reached Brentford much sooner, implying that the damage could have been worse. He therefore considered that the employees of the Regent's Canal Company responsible for the reservoir had acted appropriately and were not in any way to blame. However, he had admitted that the fracture occurred and it may be that it was knowledge of the fracture in a structure for which he was responsible which had left Mr Golden so ill.

was it knowledge of the fracture in a structure for which he was responsible which had left Mr Golden so ill?

The reports of these inquests suggest that there was a strong consensus around two matters which had, at the very least, made a serious natural disaster worse. One related to the floating timber stored in the waterway, which many people felt had contributed to the severity of the damage. But little more was made of this and the question of the timber floats was not alluded to again in later newspaper reports of the inquests.

The other matter was the question of the management of the water in the canal system at a time when the amount released was critical, given the substantial amount of water running off the land as the ice melted with the thaw. The facts were that the dam wall at Kingsbury was only a few years old and that water had been pouring over the top of it for a week prior to the disaster. It should have been strong enough to survive the pressure but, as the surveyor had revealed for the first time in public, it had fractured. He stated firmly that it could not have caused the Flood because the water released by the fracture would not have reached Brentford until after the time of the greatest damage.

His denial is not completely convincing However, PC Smith had described a very loud noise being heard at about 4am, just before the flood hit the town. This was the sound of the hugely swollen river overflowing its banks and pouring into the canal just before it hit the boats above Brentford Bridge. This sounds much more like the sudden arrival of a substantial amount of water, released all at once, than the accumulated waters of the thawing ice. The surveyor's denial is not completely convincing.

Perhaps this is why, when the jurors finally retired to consider their verdict late on the evening of 18 February, they seem to have concentrated most on the question of the reservoir. They deliberated for eleven and a half hours, before the public were re-admitted at quarter past eight on the 19th, to hear their decision. In a long and detailed statement they made clear their views on the death of young William Spruce and included a statement as to where blame might lie.

> "We find that William Spruce, being then and there on board a certain barge called the William and Henry, which was then and there floating on

certain waters called the Grand Junction Canal, it so happened that the said waters being then and there covered with ice and snow, became greatly and suddenly agitated and set in motion, and became and were greatly swollen and increased by a large influx of certain other land-waters and other waters then and there passing with great force and violence from and out of certain land springs and a certain reservoir of waters situate at Kingsbury, in the County of Middlesex, of and belonging to the company and proprietors of the Regent's Canal, and the said barge was thereby then and there driven with great force and violence to and upon a certain bank of the Grand Junction Canal, and the said William Spruce, by force and violence of the said waters, and by force and violence of a certain tiller, then and there forming a part of the said barge, was then and there forced into the waters of the said canal, to wit, at New Brentford, in the Parish of Hanwell, in the county aforesaid and was in said waters then and there immediately suffocated and drowned, of which such suffocation and drowning, the said William Spruce then and there instantly died, in the manner aforesaid.

the jurors do enforce upon the directors such an additional strength and a strict watchfulness as may prevent any future breach of the reservoir

And the jurors, upon their oaths, do feel it to be their duty to enforce upon the directors of the Regent's Canal Company, in the reconstruction of the walls of the said reservoir, lately ruptured by the ice and snow, such an additional strength, as well as an enforcement of such a strict watchfulness on the part of their servants having care of the said reservoir, as may prevent any future breach or overflow of the said waters of the reservoir, which they are of the opinion has not, on the late occasion, been sufficiently attended to."

The reporter added "The jury, whose appearance may be better conceived than described, were then after a sitting of 20 hours, discharged, and allowed to go to their homes. The above verdict will, it is believed, lay the company open to action for the amount of the damage sustained."

The Regent's Canal Company

The Grand Junction Canal had been constructed in the 1790s to link the Thames with the canal system. Maintaining the water level on busy canals was always a problem. After the opening of a branch called the Paddington Arm, between Uxbridge and the Paddington Basin in 1801, a Canal Feeder[13] channel was added around 1809-11 to carry water from the River Brent at Neasden to the canal near Harlesden. With the addition of another branch from the Basin to the Thames at Limehouse by the Regent's Canal Company, completed by 1820, the case for a reservoir was clear. It was created by constructing a dam across the Brent on the boundary between Willesden and Kingsbury parishes and completed in 1835. The reservoir is substantial, covering about 125 acres and though it is at some distance from Brentford, the link by water-flow down the valley of the Brent was significant.

The bound notebooks of the minutes of the Regent's Canal Company's managing committee survive in the Public Record Office.[14] They show that it met twice a month and dealt primarily with finance and personnel matters, property management and contracts for maintenance and construction. During the early 1840s there are several mentions (including one only a week before the flood) of the purchase of substantial quantities of rope for ice breaking and on one occasion agreement is given to boats operating exceptionally on Sundays on the Canal because their business had been so hampered by severe frost. This was clearly a period of severe winters. Reports on the matters relating to the flood appear frequently in these minutes from late January 1841 into mid 1842. Works which were carried out at the Reservoir were to entail considerable expenditure.

The flood is first mentioned at the meeting of 27 January, where a memorandum from the Deputy Chairman was considered. Mr John Golden, the company's engineer, had reported that "the Auxiliary Head [also referred to as the waste weir] of the Brent Reservoir had been carried away by the late floods" and set out what immediate action had been taken in relation to repairs. In addition, a Mr Anderson, who had been engaged by the Deputy Chairman, reported on his visit to the Reservoir. The minutes record that "he found that the Main Head [the dam] was perfectly secure, and that the

---

[13] The canal feeder channel joins the Grand Union Canal close to Waxlow Road in Harlesden.

[14] Public Record Office reference RAIL 860/38,39, 40,41

wall (of a convex form) erected by Mr Golden, was the best measure that could have been adopted to obtain a full head of water before the season passes." He suggested "with reference to the sluice cocks for letting off the waters in times of flood, that some means should be taken to get at them in case of any thing getting into the cocks to prevent their being shut", and indicating that the best time for this work to be executed would be during the next summer when the water was low in the Reservoir.

By the date of the next meeting on 10 February the company had received a letter from William Barker, the Coroner, concerning the inquest being held into the death of William Spruce. It informed them that he had adjourned the inquest to give the company the opportunity of being represented "in order that all parties might be placed on an equal footing at the next meeting". The Deputy Chairman had consulted colleagues and as a result they had engaged a lawyer to watch the proceedings and protect their interests, and a surveyor to inspect the line and progress of the flood.[15] It was also reported to this meeting that Mr Golden was very ill, but was required as a witness and as a result the inquest had been adjourned again to 18 February.

Two weeks later the committee met again. Another letter had been received from the Coroner, dated 20 February, providing a copy of the verdict of the jury on William Spruce's death and suggesting that they consider this carefully "with a view to the accomplishment of such measures as may prevent any cause of complaint in the future." A letter from Mr Golden confirmed that the Auxiliary Head or waste weir had been repaired by the erection of a wall eight bricks thick and that the Reservoir was once again full of water. He also asked, "being extremely ill from long exposure to the weather", for "leave of absence for the restoration of his health," which was approved at the discretion of the Deputy Chairman. This suggests that the committee recognised the efforts he had put into arranging rapid repairs and perhaps also the personal stress that he had been under during this crisis.

[15] Part of the lawyer's contribution was reported in *The Times*, while the surveyor's map showing the extent of the flood waters over a distance of 15 miles and 40 yards, from the Reservoir to the River Thames, was presented to the committee at its meeting on 24 March 1841.

A month later, on 24 March, the Deputy Chairman reported that he had visited the Reservoir with Mr Golden and Mr Anderson, as a result of which they proposed a series of measures. The first of these was the acquisition of a small additional piece of land just below the waste weir, to allow surface water to flow away more easily. It was agreed that a final decision on this would be made when the committee next inspected the Reservoir. Mr Golden submitted a report proposing minor works at the Reservoir. These included removing earth brought down by the flood water, which was then lying in the channel of the old River Brent. Some of this would be used in strengthening the channel by which waste water flows from the Canal Feeder to the old Brent. In addition he proposed the erection of a platform across the Main Head of the Reservoir to enable the men to pass safely during a flood and the enclosure of the valves and apparatus by a railing and gates. He also intended to level some privately-owned land which had been excavated to repair the flood damage and cover the broken brickwork with an embankment.

He (Mr Golden) was dismissed...

It is difficult to know quite what had happened to Mr Golden

All of this work was approved, for completion as soon as practicable. In April 1841 Ovid Topham was paid £297 "for sluice cocks and gearing complete, etc for the Brent Reservoir (as per contract)" and John Rutty £59.4s (£59.20p) for bricks for work at the Reservoir.

The meeting of 17 June saw an end to Mr Golden's service with the Company. He had been interviewed the previous day but was described as "too ill in body and mind" to attend the meeting. He was reported to have "acted contrary to the wishes of the Board in buying a boat and working it on the canal and employing Thomas Harding to unload boats of clay and mud and give receipts for towing and conveyance etc being services which he did not perform." He was dismissed from a post which had provided a good salary of £250 and a house. No further detail about him appears in the minutes. Mr Radford was taken on as acting engineer for the time being while they advertised for a replacement; he appears later to have won the post.

It is difficult to know quite what had happened to Mr Golden. He appeared to have acted quickly and very responsibly at the time of the fracture of the dam and done all he might have been expected to do. Indeed, he personally had probably acted beyond the call of duty during the extremely bad weather. The inquiries made in connection with his failure to attend the inquest had

The dam at the Brent Reservoir after rebuilding, photographed in the 1880s (Brent Archive)

confirmed that he was genuinely ill and he was sufficiently well thought of to be allowed leave of absence by the Company for several months. He seemed to have done something foolish enough to result in his dismissal, and it is not made clear whether this was before he became ill or after the Flood when he was ill "in body and in mind". The Company's minutes contain no more about him.

The company held its 14 July meeting at the Brent Reservoir, accompanied by Mr Radford and Mr Anderson. They inspected the Reservoir and Feeder and considered all the matters which had been drawn to their attention at earlier meetings. They selected a site for the Reservoir Cottage to the north of the dam and instructed Mr Radford to obtain tenders for its construction. They also required him to arrange for the water to be pumped out of the basin of the Main Head to enable a report to be prepared on its condition. He reported to the meeting two weeks later that this was undamaged by the flood and small maintenance works had been completed. In addition, tenders had been received for the cottage and the contract was awarded to Samuel Sowter, at a cost of £180.12s (£180.60p)

A year later a group of directors again visited the site and instructed Radford and Anderson to prepare plans and estimates for improvement works "to carry off flood water in the future." Mr Anderson claimed that he "has no doubt that the new waste weir, when completed according to his plans, would be quite sufficient to carry off all the Flood Waters of the Brent Reservoir" and estimated the cost at £1,700. In August 1842, they met at the Company's cottage at Kingsbury after an inspection of the works in progress. A bill for just over £8 for repainting the cottage, perhaps in anticipation of the visit, was paid on 10 August. The contract for major works to the waste weir at the Reservoir was awarded to Messrs W & T Stewart who had worked for the Company on a number of other contracts. They were paid £306 on account on 21 September 1842, and then staged payments until its completion in early 1843.

Though *The Times* reporter mentioned the possibility that the inquest verdict may lay the company open to claims for compensation for damage, only a few are mentioned in the minutes. On 24 March the company rejected a claim from the Hanwell Lunatic Asylum for repairs to its fencing which had been washed away by the flood. On 19 May a claim from Messrs John and E Walker

the company was behaving…as if the Flood had nothing to do with them

In private…the directors were at the very least rattled by the disaster and certainly determined not to be blamed in future

for the sum of £238 for damage to a large quantity of cast-iron borings "said to have been occasioned by the bursting of the reservoir" was considered. However, the Deputy Chairman had already written a reply indicating that "the public investigation had so fully proved that no damage was or could have been occasioned by anything which happened at the Company's Reservoir that the claim in question could not for one moment be entertained by the Committee" and the committee agreed.

In January 1842, a full year after the disaster, a letter from Mr G Clark was considered, applying on behalf of Mr Norris, the Brentford tanner, for compensation for damage occasioned to him by the bursting of the Reservoir. Once again the Deputy Chairman had already written rejecting the claim. So despite the verdict on William Spruce, the company was behaving – to the outside world at least – as if the Flood had nothing to do with them. In private, the amount of time at meetings devoted to considering improvements to the dam and the levels of expenditure involved over several years suggest that the directors were at the very least rattled by the disaster and certainly determined not to be blamed in future.

Mr Golden and his successor, Mr Radford, were clearly capable engineers but may not have been good managers of people. Much emphasis was placed on improving the design of the structure and equipment of the Regent's Canal and its Reservoir, but little was said about the workers. Perhaps everything usually ran smoothly, but in November 1841 the committee considered a petition from the lock-keepers who supervised the St Pancras and City Road locks. There were only two of them at each of these locks and they were obliged to work 36 hours at a stretch, only resting on alternate nights, because of the inadequate level of staffing. Two new assistant lock-keepers were now to be appointed to support them.

Recognising the importance of skilled men in ensuring smooth running and avoiding disaster must have contributed to the decision to build the Reservoir Cottage. The occupant would be responsible for the close monitoring and regulation of the water level, managing the amount flowing through the Canal Feeder to maintain safety. (A slightly more sophisticated version of this system, with the addition of an electric bell to warn the attendant that the water had reached a certain level, continued well into the 20th century, though now the control of the water level is automatic.) These changes suggest that the Regent's Canal Company had accepted responsibility for improving its future management of the reservoir, even though it continued to claim that it was not responsible for the flooding of Brentford.

Postscript

As I write in May 2002 the site of the tannery and adjoining properties beside the Brent and the Canal, and across the High Street from St Lawrence's Church, is being developed for waterside housing as part of the regeneration of Brentford. The archaeological excavations here in the summer of 2001 revealed that successive brick revetments had been built to strengthen the bank on the southern edge of the old channel of the Brent at this point. This was the scene of the greatest overflow of the floodwater in 1841 and of the worst damage.

There had been another serious flood in Brentford in 1682, apparently in the same location as St Lawrence's Church suffered damage. The Rev Daniel Lysons, writing just over a century later, describes it as follows

> "a very violent storm of rain, accompanied by thunder and lightning, caused a sudden flood, which did great damage to the town of Brentford. The whole place was overflown; boats rowed up and down the streets, and several houses and other buildings were carried away by the force of the waters. . . It appears also that the walls of the church-yard and the pews in the church received considerable damage."

Lysons says that a document held by Col Clitherow shows that the losses incurred as a result were estimated at £718. He also quotes from the Churchwardens' Accounts an entry for 26 April 1682:

> "Paid the watermen in bread, beer and brandy that brought their boats to save the people from the flood this day, 6 shillings...
>
> Paid for cleaning water out of the church, mops, etc, 9 shillings".

Other, less serious, floods have occurred since 1841. For example, in 1898 a small humped brick bridge across the lock just north of the Brentford Bridge had to be replaced after flood damage and postcards of the 1903 flood show water pouring over the top of the closed lock-gates.

Some comfort might also be obtained from the reports in the house journal of the British Waterways Board on the effective handling of a serious threat of flooding in 1987. This publication reported on difficulties faced by British Waterways staff as a result of the hurricane force winds and very heavy rain which hit South-east England in mid-October of that year. One of the main problems was the management of water levels at the Brent Reservoir. Here

Postcard views of the June 1903 Flood. **Above**, the gauging lock above Brentford Bridge with water overflowing its gates. This lock was rebuilt in this double form after the old single lock was severely damaged in the floods of 1898. **Below**, the turbulent water has reached the level of the bridge and overflowed the banks of the canal.

the water rose rapidly and it was found necessary to open the sluice gates to approximately five feet, a level which had not been recorded for many years previously. This prevented the automatic siphons from cutting in, which they would have done if the level of the water in the reservoir had risen to one foot above the level of the run-off weir. While this would have preserved the integrity of the reservoir, three times as much water would have been discharged down the Brent.

The vigilant staff made a careful judgment about the best course of action and could rely on flood prevention works along the Brent executed by the Greater London Council and the Thames Water Authority in the early 1980s. Though their actions avoided flooding in Ealing, the heavy water flows caused by opening the sluices did cause some damage to the canal at Brentford but they did not inundate the town.

Serious flooding in other areas of England in the winters of 2000, 2001 and 2002 has further heightened our awareness of the risk of building in river flood plains. During the period of floods in 2000 local residents observed that the substantial flow of water from the upper reaches of the Thames meant that, even at low tide, the foreshore at Brentford was rarely uncovered. We also known that the Thames Barrier was frequently closed during this period to minimise the impact of the incoming tide. But Brentford was not flooded, either from the Thames or the Brent.

The improvements to the dam and the canals carried out since 1841-3, the recognition that close supervision is needed in times of risk and the substantial late twentieth century flood prevention works along the Brent and the Thames seem to have combined to keep Brentford safe.

Brentford & Chiswick Local History Society

The Society was established in 1958 to promote interest and research in the history of Brentford & Chiswick, then combined in one borough. It meets once a month, for talks on local topics, from September to May. It also organises summer outings, usually to historic sites and museums which have something to contribute to our understanding of our own area, puts on occasional talks, walks and exhibitions and supports a publications programme. The Brentford & Chiswick Local History Journal is published every spring, free to members. The Society also keeps a comprehensive stock of local publications for sale.

New members are always welcome. Programme details can usually be obtained from the libraries in Brentford and Chiswick or from the Society at 25 Hartington Road, Chiswick, London W4 3TL.

Val Bott is a museum curator who has run local museums in four London Boroughs and worked as a government adviser on museums. She has been a member of the Brentford & Chiswick Local History Society since the mid-1970s and has written articles for their Journal. She chairs the co-ordinating committee for the annual West London Local History Conference and is honorary treasurer to the Thames Explorer Trust.